EXTREME SURVIVAL
SPACE

Angela Royston

Chrysalis Children's Books

EXTREME FACTS

Look for the Earth and Space Shuttle in boxes like this. Here you will find extra facts, stories and information about space.

B514158

| Bertrams | |
| JN | £5.99 |

First published in the UK in 2003 by
Chrysalis Children's Books
An imprint of Chrysalis Books Group Plc
The Chrysalis Building, Bramley Road, London W10 6SP

Copyright © Chrysalis Books Group Plc 2003

Design and editorial production
Bender Richardson White, Uxbridge

ISBN 1 84138 701 0 (hb)
ISBN 1 84458 455 0 (pb)

British Library Cataloguing in Publication Data for this book is available from the British Library.

Printed in China

10 9 8 7 6 5 4 3 2 1

Acknowledgements

We wish to thank the following individuals and organizations for their help and assistance and for supplying material in their collections:
CORBIS Corporation/Images: pages 10, 12, 13, and 19 top (all Roger Ressmeyer/CORBIS), 19 bottom (CORBIS), 20 (Bettmann/CORBIS), 20–21 (Denis Scott/CORBIS), 23 (CORBIS). Ecoscene: pages 13 top. NASA/JPL: pages 1, 7 top, 7 bottom, 9 left, 11 bottom, 16, 17 top, 21, 22, 24 top, 24 bottom, 26. Oxford Scientific Films Photo Library: pages 6, 8, 11 top, 14, 15 top, 15 bottom, 17 bottom, 18, 20, 23 bottom and 27 (all NASA/JPL). Still Pictures: pages 4–5 (DERA), 5 (Nick White), 29 (Vincent Decorde).
Cover photos: Front: Oxford Scientific Films Photo Library/NASA. Back: NASA/JPL
Illustrations: Alex Pang
Diagrams: Stefan Chabluk.

Editorial Manager: Joyce Bentley
Project Editor: Lionel Bender
Text Editor: Clare Hibbert
Design and Make-up: Ben White
Picture Research: Cathy Stastny
Production: Kim Richardson
Consultant: John Stidworthy

We have checked the records in this book but new ones are often added.

▼ An artist's impression of how a giant, solar-powered space station might look someday (see pages 18–19).

CONTENTS

◀ A computer-generated image of the planet Saturn and its moons (see pages 4–7).

WHAT IS SPACE?

Space is everything outside the Earth's atmosphere – the layer of air around our planet. It is the most difficult place for living things to survive because there is no oxygen or water, two essentials for life.

Space is vast. Our Solar System – the Sun and all the planets that circle around it – is just a tiny part of space. Beyond it are billions of stars, galaxies, black holes and all the empty space in between.

▶ Nine planets, including Earth, circle or orbit the Sun. Some of the planets have moons that circle round them. Here the planets are shown in the order of their distance from the Sun. A photo of the Earth is shown opposite.

Pluto

Neptune

Saturn

Uranus

Jupiter

Mars

Mercury

Earth

Venus

Sun – the star at the centre of the Solar System (Here it is shown at a much smaller scale).

Scientists have sent unmanned spacecraft (ones without people on board) to explore the other planets in our Solar System. So far they have found no place where people, animals or plants have all the essentials for life. People cannot live in space unless they take with them all the things they need to survive. This means that living things can only survive in space inside a spacesuit, spacecraft or space station.

TOO FAR TO IMAGINE

Distances in space are so big they are measured in light years. This is the distance light travels in a year (9 000 000 000 000 km). It takes about four years for light to reach us from Alpha Centauri C, our next closest star after the Sun. Light from other stars takes millions of years to reach Earth!

▲ The Earth moves through space like every other planet. So far, Earth is the only place where we know for sure that life exists.

▶ You can see furthest into space at night. In the centre of this picture is a comet, a lump of icy space rock. Comets orbit stars along paths that regulary take them close to planets.

Parts of space are too extreme even for spacecraft. The Sun and other stars are so hot that they would burn up any craft that came within thousands of kilometres. Black holes, too, are impossible to get close to. Any craft would be sucked in and crushed.

OTHER WORLDS

The Moon is the only other world that astronauts have visited. But we know what the planets are like because scientists have sent unmanned space probes to all except one of them.

A space probe beams back information about the places it visits. Probes have landed on Mars and Venus, the nearest planets to Earth. And they have flown close to the huge outer planets – Jupiter, Saturn, Uranus and Neptune. Pluto, the farthest planet, has not been explored yet.

▼ The Moon is Earth's nearest neighbour. Edwin 'Buzz' Aldrin and Neil Armstrong became the first of 12 astronauts to have landed on the Moon, more than 30 years ago. Spacecraft can reach the Moon in days, but it takes years to reach the distant planets – too long for a safe manned flight.

CHANGE OF AIR

Venus's atmosphere is mostly carbon dioxide. If there were plants there, they could slowly change this into oxygen so that other forms of life could survive there. The problem is that no plant could grow on Venus – it is too hot!

◀ On Mars much of the ground is covered with rocks and boulders. The highest mountains rise to more than three times the height of Mount Everest (8848m).

Except for Mercury and Pluto, which have almost no atmosphere, the planets are surrounded by gases, but none have enough oxygen to support life. The large outer planets are balls of gas and liquid with no land. The inner planets are rocky like Earth. Mercury and Venus are close to the Sun and blistering hot. Mars is further away and freezing cold.

▲ A representation of *Cassini-Huygens* flying past Saturn in 1997. The probe identified the gases in the planet's atmosphere.

Despite the conditions on Mars, scientists think that simple forms of life, such as bacteria, might be found there. If the planet ever had water, there may be fossils of past life, too. Since space is so vast, most people believe that life must exist somewhere else in the universe.

GOING UP

A layer of air clings round the Earth. The higher you go above the ground, the thinner the air becomes. At just over 500 km, air fades away and space begins.

Air is made of gases, mostly nitrogen and oxygen. The layer of air closest to the Earth is called the troposphere. This contains about three-quarters of all the gases. It is also the layer that produces all the clouds, rain and weather.

The next layer up is the stratosphere. This contains too little oxygen for life to exist. Within the stratosphere is a band of air called the ozone layer. This is Earth's sunscreen. It absorbs heat and dangerous rays from the Sun.

▶ The US Space Shuttle takes off. The spacecraft is attached to its huge fuel tank. Two booster rockets help to lift the shuttle into space.

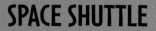

SPACE SHUTTLE
The US Space Shuttle is several times taller than a house. The spacecraft is launched with rockets. The fuel tank can only be used once, but the craft can be used 100 times.

Above the stratosphere, you eventually reach the outer layers of Earth's atmosphere. Here, the air is so thin that the Sun heats it to 2000°C.

Gravity is the force that holds Earth's atmosphere and stops it floating off into space. It is the same force that makes things fall to Earth – and that aeroplanes and spacecraft must overcome in order to fly. Rockets are the gravity-defying engines that lift spacecraft into space.

▶ **The Earth's atmosphere consists of five main layers (with names from Greek words, such as *sphaira* for ball and *mesos* meaning middle). Above the ozone layer, the atmosphere is filled with lethal rays – radiation – from the Sun.**

▼ **The Lockheed *SR-71 Blackbird* can fly high in the stratosphere, close to space, 30 km above the ground and at a speed of 3200 km/h.**

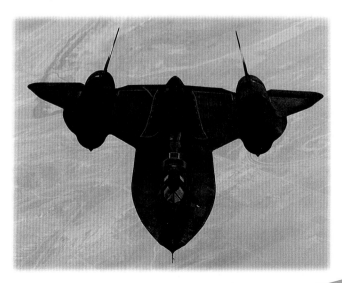

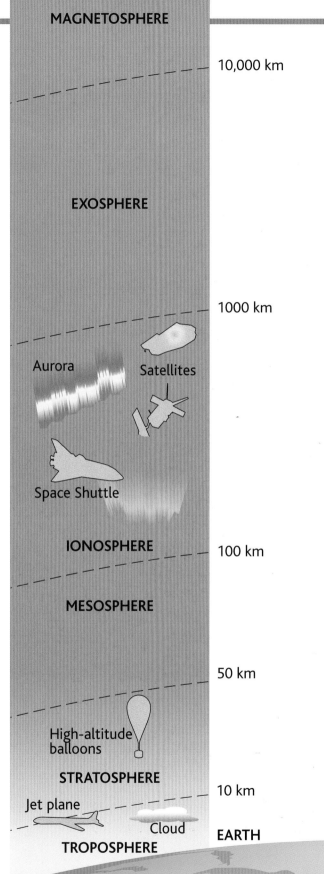

MAGNETOSPHERE

10,000 km

EXOSPHERE

1000 km

Aurora   Satellites

Space Shuttle

IONOSPHERE   100 km

MESOSPHERE

50 km

High-altitude balloons

STRATOSPHERE

10 km

Jet plane

Cloud   EARTH

TROPOSPHERE

ORBITING THE EARTH

Astronauts spend their time in space orbiting the Earth. Some spend a few days. Others stay there for many months. But all astronauts experience the extraordinary conditions of living in space.

In space, there is no pull of gravity keeping astronauts grounded. They float, weightlessly, around the inside of the spacecraft. They use their feet and hands to push themselves off the walls and then float to where they want to go. There is no upside-down in space! The feeling is so strange that astronauts often feel sick at first.

▼ In space, objects and astronauts do not experience gravity – the invisible force that pulls everything to the ground. If astronauts want to stay in one place, they must strap themselves in.

FLOATING OBJECTS
Everything is weightless in space. If you let go of an object, such as a carton of juice or a notepad, it floats away! To keep the spacecraft tidy, everything has to be put away or fastened down.

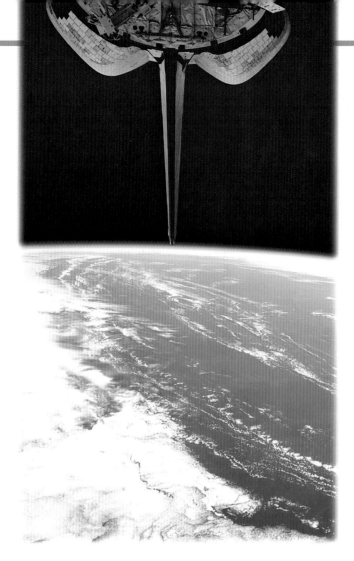

The Shuttle spacecraft orbits the Earth every 90 minutes. Each time it turns away from the Sun, the astronauts are plunged into darkness. So every 90 minutes, they pass from sunlight into darkness and then back again into sunlight. The temperature outside the spacecraft changes from baking hot on the sunny side to freezing cold on the dark side. Solar panels make electricity to heat or cool the inside of the spacecraft and so keep the astronauts at a comfortable temperature. Electricity powers other machines too, such as one that makes oxygen for the astronauts to breathe.

◄ **Astronauts have amazing views of the clouds, oceans and land below them. This view of Earth from the Shuttle shows the North Pole region.**

▼ **The large flat panels on this space station are solar panels. They collect energy from the Sun and change it into electricity.**

LIVING IN SPACE

Imagine being weightless. It sounds fantastic, but it gives astronauts many problems. Scientists have had to devise special ways for astronauts to eat, drink, rest, exercise – and go to the toilet – in space.

Space is vast and silent, but living in a spacecraft is noisy and cramped. The spacecraft is filled with the humming of machines. These keep the air fresh, make light and heat, and keep the spacecraft on course. Although the living area is small, it includes storage space for food, bunks for sleeping, a toilet and a shower.

▼ By flying high in an aircraft it is possible to create the same conditions as weightlessness in space. This trainee astronaut's hair is certainly weightless!

TABLE MANNERS

Astronauts eat some food with their fingers but they use cutlery as well. It is quite a skill keeping food on the spoon! Liquids are even harder to handle. Most drinks come in bags, to be drunk through a straw.

Astronauts do not prepare their own meals. They take trays of food that have been prepared on Earth, or dried foods. The astronauts just have to add water and heat it up. Scientists have invented special toilets and showers for astronauts to use in space. The liquid and solid wastes are dried and stored to be brought back to Earth.

Light and dark changes often as the spacecraft orbits the Earth, so the astronauts make their own day and night. When the time comes to sleep, they cover the windows to keep the cabin dark. Their sleeping bags are strapped to their bunks. Not even astronauts like to float around while they are asleep!

▲ The astronauts keep in constant contact with Mission Control on the ground. This photograph is the control centre at NASA – the US space agency – in Houston, Texas. NASA stands for National Aeronautics and Space Administration.

▶ Eating lunch in weightless conditions. Inside the craft, astronauts wear normal clothing.

SPACEWALKS

Sometimes an astronaut leaves the safety of the spacecraft for a spacewalk, to carry out an experiment, take photographs or repair a satellite. Then he or she is exposed to the Sun's powerful rays and other dangers.

Space is a hazardous place. There is no oxygen to breathe and the temperature changes from very cold to burning hot. That is why the astronaut wears a spacesuit when outside the craft. The suit has its own air supply, and it keeps the body at the right temperature and pressure. The spacesuit also protects from most, but not all, of the harmful rays of the Sun.

▼ Two astronauts work on the outside of the Space Shuttle. They are both tied or tethered to the spacecraft. No astronaut spends more than a few hours outside the craft or does many spacewalks as the Sun's rays can harm the human body permanently.

14

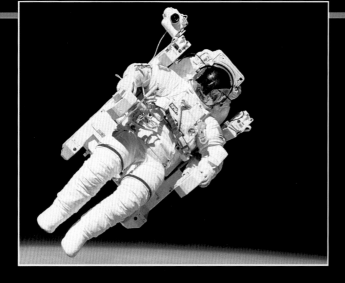

◀ **This astronaut is wearing an MMU (manned manoeuvring unit). Its jet power will keep him from floating away, so he does not need to be tethered to the spacecraft.**

Visor and oxygen mask

Air pack and communications

Mission Control link-up pack

PEACE AND QUIET

It can take hours to repair a satellite but, after the noise inside the spacecraft, the spacewalk is silent and peaceful. There is no sound in space, because there is no air to carry sound waves.

Gloves

Another danger to astronauts outside spacecraft is flying objects. Space may look empty, but it is full of bits of rock, called meteoroids. A strike from one of these could be fatal.

Astronauts on a spacewalk have to be careful to stay close to the craft. If they floated off, they could drift forever. Astronauts often tie themselves to the craft while they are working. Or they put on jet-powered spacesuits, called MMUs, so they can control their direction.

Tube to remove body wastes.

◀ **A spacesuit provides everything an astronaut needs to survive for a short time in space.**

WALKING ON THE MOON

The Moon is the furthest place that any people have been from Earth – 385 000 km. Apollo spacecraft made six missions to the Moon between 1969 and 1972. The first Moon landing was on 20 July 1969.

Each Apollo spacecraft had a smaller craft on board, called the lunar module. The lunar module could ferry two astronauts to the Moon. A third astronaut stayed on board the main spacecraft, orbiting the Moon.

Millions of people watched the first Moon landing on television. The two astronauts put on their spacesuits and stepped out on to the Moon's surface. They walked and jumped about and collected samples of rocks and soil. They and other astronauts, who followed them in later missions, set up instruments to record any changes on the Moon, such as 'moonquakes'.

▼ This astronaut is scooping up soil from the Moon. The camera around his neck is filming what he is doing.

UNCHANGING WORLD

The last astronaut left the Moon in December 1972, but nothing has changed since. The Moon has no weather, so the astronauts' scientific instruments are undisturbed. Moon probe images show their footprints remain intact and items they left have not rotted.

When the astronauts were ready to leave the Moon, they fired a rocket in the lunar module. This was one of the most dangerous moments in the mission. If the rocket engine did not work, the astronauts would have been stranded. Luckily this did not happen. Each time the lunar module rejoined the spacecraft and all the astronauts returned safely to Earth.

▼ The lunar module was home to the first astronauts – Edwin Aldrin and Neil Armstrong – for the day they spent on the Moon.

▼ In the Apollo 11 spacecraft, astronaut Michael Collins stayed in orbit while his two companions landed on the Moon. The astronauts stayed in touch by radio.

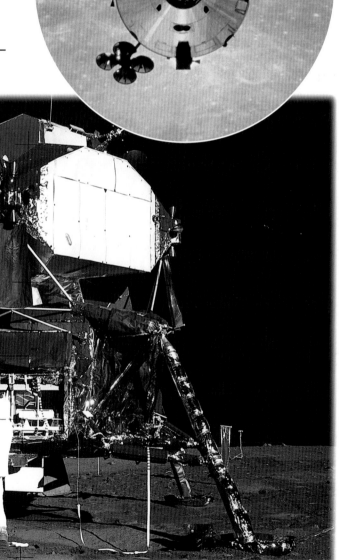

SPACE STATION LIFE

A space station is much larger than a spacecraft. It provides a space base where astronauts and space scientists can live and work for months at a time.

LONG STINTS IN SPACE
The Russian space station *Mir* was designed to see how well astronauts can live for long periods in space. Several astronauts stayed on *Mir* for more than a year. Today, crews usually spend about five months on a space station.

A space station is too large to be built on Earth and then launched. The pieces are taken up a bit at a time and the station is assembled as it orbits in space. Each part locks into the next, like a huge construction kit. Astronauts on spacewalks check the construction.

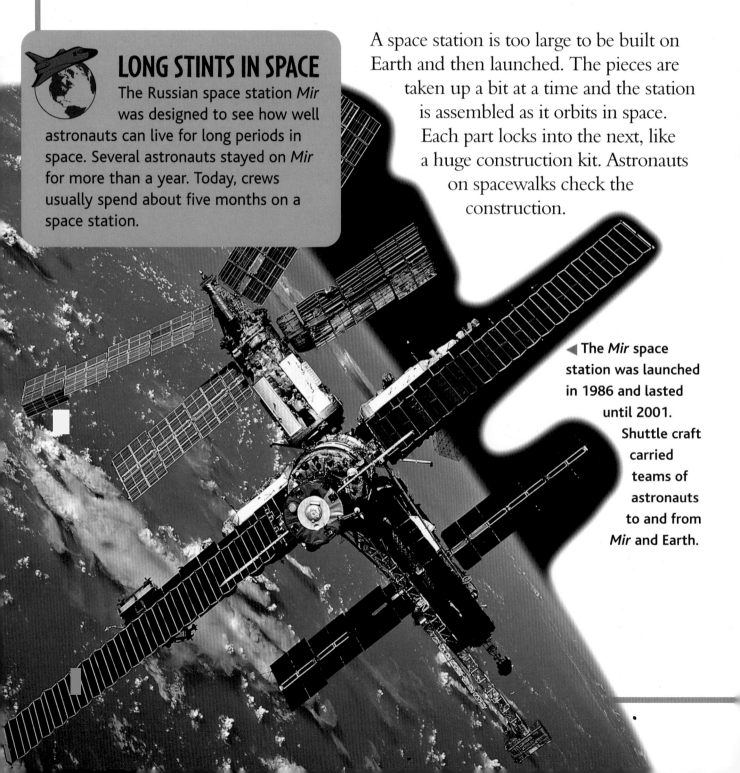

◀ The *Mir* space station was launched in 1986 and lasted until 2001. Shuttle craft carried teams of astronauts to and from *Mir* and Earth.

▲ Inside the *International Space Station*. Sixteen different countries teamed up to build it.

▶ Weightlessness makes muscles weak. Astronauts need to exercise on special machines.

Astronauts and space scientists work hard during their time in the space station. They carry out many different experiments. Some experiments are related to living in space. One of the first was to see how well plants can grow without gravity to draw their roots down. If astronauts ever travel long distances, to Mars for example, plants will help to provide fresh food.

Other experiments test the effect of being in space on the astronauts' own bodies. They measure, for example, how it affects their lungs and their muscles. Even with exercise, their muscles become weak since there is no gravity to work against.

While all this is going on, the astronauts must keep a constant watch on the space station's systems and communicate with Mission Control. Computers control all the systems and TV screens display the status, or condition, of the machinery.

SPACE ACCIDENTS

Space missions are carefully planned, but even so things can go wrong. When this happens, Mission Control on Earth helps and advises astronauts. But astronauts also have to rely on their wits to survive.

The most dangerous situation is when a hole in a spacecraft allows the air to leak out. Without air, astronauts will die in minutes. In 1970, one of the Moon missions – *Apollo 13* – had just this problem. An oxygen tank exploded in the main spacecraft and the air escaped. The astronauts squeezed into the lunar module and sealed it off from the rest of the spacecraft. Then they headed for home. To land their craft, they put on spacesuits and crawled back into the main spacecraft. They survived the mission.

BURNING SHUTTLE
On 1 February 2003, Space Shuttle *Columbia* burned up on re-entry into the Earth's atmosphere. The likely cause was that a heat shield protecting the craft had been damaged on take-off. All the crew were killed.

◀ On 28 January 1986 Space Shuttle *Challenger* exploded soon after take-off. Fuel leaking from the rockets ignited. All seven astronauts on board were killed.

In 1997 a similar situation arose on *Mir*. An unmanned spacecraft bringing supplies from Earth crashed into part of *Mir*. The astronauts had only a short time to stop air leaking from the whole station. Working fast, they managed to seal off the damaged area. Their problems were not over, however. The same accident damaged some of the solar panels, leaving *Mir* short of power for many weeks.

◀ An impression of a meteoroid burning up as it enters the Earth's atmosphere. As it falls, it could strike a spacecraft or astronaut on a spacewalk!

▼ *Mir's* solar panels were damaged when a supply craft hit the space station. Space 'junk' from worn out spacecraft can also hit a space station.

LANDING

Returning from space and landing back on Earth is not easy. American astronauts come and go from the International Space Station in the Shuttle. Russian astronauts – called cosmonauts – use *Soyuz* crafts.

The people at Mission Control carefully plan the speed and angle at which a spacecraft re-enters Earth's atmosphere. They have to make sure that the craft lands where they want it to. First, the spacecraft slows down so that it drops into the atmosphere. As it falls through the air, friction between the air and the craft slows it further. At the same time the friction makes the underside red-hot. Spacecraft have a heat shield that protects the astronauts and the rest of the craft.

▼ Divers wave triumphantly as they reach the *Apollo 9* spacecraft after it landed in the Atlantic Ocean in 1969.

Early American spacecraft dropped into the sea, where they floated until they were picked up by a waiting boat. Before the spacecraft hit the surface, parachutes opened so it landed gently. The *Soyuz* craft still come down in a similar way, but drop onto land rather than water. The Space Shuttle, however, glides down to Earth and lands like an aeroplane. As it touches down, a parachute opens to help slow it to a stop.

NO ENGINES

The Shuttle looks like a huge plane as it comes in to land. But unlike an aeroplane, it does not have engines to control its descent and help it brake! It falls from space and then glides on to the runway.

▼ The Space Shuttle *Atlantis* touches down. The open parachute helps the spacecraft brake and stop.

▲ Home at last! Using a mechanical arm, the Shuttle astronauts are brought to the ground from the spacecraft .

THE FUTURE

Space scientists are planning future missions. They want to send astronauts to Mars. They are also looking for signs of life in space, perhaps on Mars or on one of the moons of Jupiter.

Mars is the only possible planet for a manned mission. Water may exist there, and where there is water, living things can survive. Mercury and Venus are too hot and Jupiter and Saturn are too far away. Space scientists have made detailed plans for a Mars mission. The journey would take six months and the astronauts would live in their spacecraft after they landed. They would need extra living area and nuclear-powered units to provide electricity, so those would have to be sent ahead.

▲ Astronauts on Mars will have to wear spacesuits outside the spacecraft. They will use a vehicle called a rover to explore the planet.

▼ A mission to Mars will be expensive and difficult. These are the units that space scientists have designed for astronauts to live and work in on Mars.

One reason scientists are keen to send people to Mars is that they hope to find evidence of life there. They used to think life could not exist without oxygen, water and a reasonable temperature. But scientists have recently discovered simple living things in unexpected places! They have found bacteria that can exist without oxygen, and plants that can survive extreme cold. So why, they ask, should life not also exist on Mars?

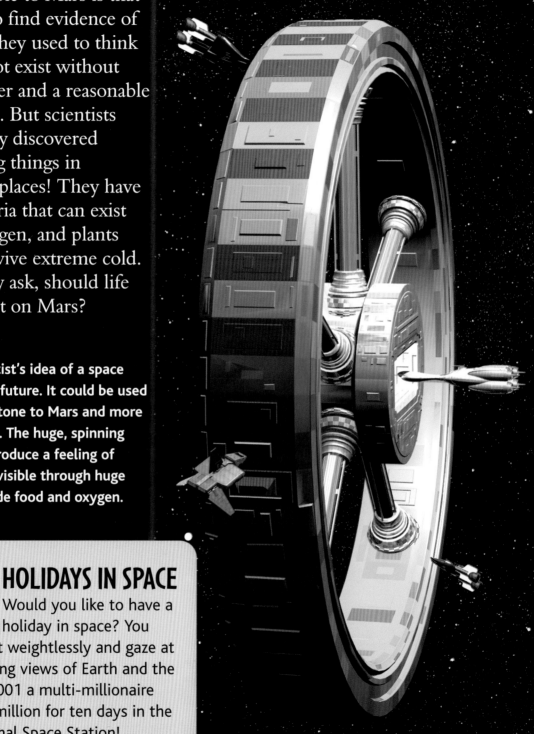

▶ This is an artist's idea of a space station for the future. It could be used as a stepping stone to Mars and more distant planets. The huge, spinning wheel would produce a feeling of gravity. Farms visible through huge windows provide food and oxygen.

HOLIDAYS IN SPACE

Would you like to have a holiday in space? You could float weightlessly and gaze at the stunning views of Earth and the stars. In 2001 a multi-millionaire paid £14 million for ten days in the International Space Station!

SPACE: FACTS

THE SUN

The Sun is a huge ball of burning gas. Eggs fry at 120°C, but the temperature on the Sun's surface is 5500°C! The centre of the Sun is even hotter – an amazing 15 000 000°C.

BEST POSITION

Life on Earth relies on the Sun for light, warmth and energy. The Earth is about 150 000 000 km from the Sun – just the right distance to support life. Mars, which is farther from the Sun, is probably too cold – although it might have some very simple, tough life forms.

MILKY WAY

The Sun is one star in a galaxy called the Milky Way. The Milky Way contains hundreds of billions of stars and, some astronomers believe, a black hole at the centre.

BIGGEST PLANET

Jupiter is the biggest planet in our Solar System. You could fit more than 1000 Earths inside it.

▼ This artist's impression shows the probe landing in 1999 from the joint European and US *Cassini-Huygens* spacecraft on to Titan, one of Saturn's moons.

FIRST SPACECRAFT

The first craft to orbit the Earth was the Russian satellite *Sputnik 1*. It was put into orbit by a rocket launched from Baikonur in Kazakhstan on 4 October 1957.

FIRST SPACEMAN

Cosmonaut (Russian astronaut) Yuri Gagarin was launched into space on 12 April 1961. He orbited the Earth once in a spacecraft called *Vostok 1*.

FIRST SPACEWOMAN

Cosmonaut Valentina Tereshkova was the first woman to travel into space. On 16 June 1963 her spaceship *Vostok 6* was launched. She stayed in space for three days, orbiting the Earth 48 times.

FIRST MOON LANDING

The first men to land on the Moon were Neil Armstrong and Edwin 'Buzz' Aldrin, on 20 July 1969. As Armstrong's feet touched the surface he said "That's one small step for man, one giant leap for mankind".

SPACE SHUTTLE

The first Space Shuttle was launched in April 1981. The crew were John Young and Robert Crippen. The seventh launch included Sally Ride, the first woman to fly in the Shuttle.

◀ An astronaut on a spacewalk uses a special tool to make a repair.

SPACE: SUMMARY

Space presents living things with conditions ranging from lack of oxygen and water to radiation and temperatures ranging from far below freezing to fierce heat that melts any rock or metal.

Plants and animals cannot survive naturally in this extreme environment. But they, and people, can survive in space inside spacesuits, spacecraft or space stations. Astronauts need fresh supplies of air, water and food and ways of getting rid of their body wastes. They need to be sheltered from the extreme temperatures, rays from the Sun or being hit by meteoroids or by space junk – the remains of old spacecraft. And they need a way of getting back to Earth.

▼ Japanese scientists are planning to build a hotel for space tourists. In this painting, a futuristic space ferry is bringing back to Earth holiday-makers who have spent a week in the orbiting hotel.

28

SPACE: ON THE WEB

If you are able to use the Internet, you can search the World Wide Web to find out more about space. Remember that websites can change, so if you cannot find all the sites shown below, do not worry. You can find more websites via a search engine by typing in keywords such as 'planets', 'Solar System' or 'Space Shuttle'.

http://starchild.gsfc.nasa.gov/docs/StarChild/ StarChild.html

This site has been especially designed for kids and gives information about the Moon, the planets and the universe, as well as about space travel.

▼ **The bright light in the centre of this photo is the Andromeda galaxy. It is two million light years away.**

International Space Station
http://spaceflight.nasa.gov/station/

This site tells you about the International Space Station, how it was built and what is happening there now. It tells you what experiments are currently being carried out.

Space Food
http://lsda.jsc.nasa.gov/kids/L&W/ eatdrink.htm

This is one of many sites provided by NASA. It tells you all about how food is prepared for space and how it is heated up and eaten. This site is linked to others that tell you about all aspects of living in space.

Mars Mission
http://nssdc.gsfc.nasa.gov/planetary/planets/ marspage.html

This NASA site tells you all about the possibility of a mission to Mars. It describes the problems of making this momentous journey – and how they could be solved.

European Space Programme
http://www.esa.int/export/esaCP/index.html

This site gives you information about the multi-national European Space Agency: its flights, history, images of Earth and details of jobs available for trainee astronauts and space scientists.

SPACE: WORDS

This glossary explains some of the words used in this book that you might not have seen before.

Astronaut
a person who travels into space.

Atmosphere
a layer of gases that surrounds a planet or moon.

Bacteria
simple, one-celled life forms.

Black hole
a burnt-out star with very strong gravity that sucks everything in, even light.

Carbon dioxide
one of the gases in the air. It is breathed out by living things.

Friction
a force created when two surfaces rub together.

Galaxy
a group of millions or billions of stars.

Gravity
the force of attraction between any two objects. Earth's gravity pulls objects in and stops them floating off into space.

Lunar module
the part of the *Apollo* spacecraft that separated from the main craft to land on the Moon.

Meteoroid
a lump of rock that travels through space. Occasionally meteoroids hit the Earth.

Mission Control
people on Earth who control a space mission or voyage with the help of computers.

MMU (manned manoeuvring unit)
a jet-powered spacesuit.

NASA (the National Aeronautics and Space Agency)
organization responsible for American activities in space.

Orbit
to circle round something; the path followed by a planet, moon, satellite etc. around another object in space.

▶ This painting shows a family on a futuristic space journey to the distant planets.

Oxygen

one of the gases in the air. Plants and animals need oxygen to survive.

Planet

a huge, natural object that orbits a star, just as Earth (a planet) orbits the Sun (a star).

Pressure

a force that presses on a surface.

Satellite

an object that orbits a larger object. The Moon is a satellite of the Earth.

Solar panel

a device that turns energy from the Sun into electricity.

Solar System

the Sun and all the objects that orbit it, including the nine planets and their moons.

▶ When the Space Shuttle is in orbit, the doors of the cargo bay (central area) are kept open to help control the temperature of the craft. This cutaway shows the living area (in the front) and rockets, too.

Spacecraft

a vehicle that travels through space.

Space probe

an unmanned spacecraft used for exploring parts of space.

Space Shuttle

the US reusable spacecraft.

Space station

a space 'building', where astronauts can live for months at a time.

Spacesuit

protective clothing that provides air, heat and other essentials to astronauts.

Unmanned

without a crew.

Weightless

floating, because there is little or no gravity to keep you down.

INDEX